40
PRAYERS

FOR YOUR
QUIET TIME

40 PRAYERS

FOR YOUR QUIET TIME

**Prayers for the
Church or home**

DAVID CLOWES

DAVID C COOK

transforming lives together

40 PRAYERS FOR YOUR QUIET TIME
Published by David C Cook
4050 Lee Vance Drive
Colorado Springs, CO 80918 U.S.A.

Integrity Music Limited, a Division of David C Cook
Brighton, East Sussex BN1 2RE, England

The graphic circle C logo is a registered trademark of David C Cook.

The website addresses recommended throughout this book
are offered as a resource to you. These websites are not
intended in any way to be or imply an endorsement on the
part of David C Cook, nor do we vouch for their content.

ISBN 978-0-8307-8233-8
eISBN 978-0-8307-8241-3

The Team: Ian Matthews, Jack Campbell,
Jo Stockdale, Susan Murdock
Cover Design: Pete Barnsley

Printed in the United Kingdom
First Edition 2020

1 2 3 4 5 6 7 8 9 10

090120

CONTENTS

INTRODUCTION

Having published *500 Prayers for All Occasions* and *500 More Prayers for All Occasions* I was asked to develop a new series of books of prayer for use in small groups or in the home.

There are at least forty prayers in each of these books based around a single theme. Most of the content comes from my first two books of prayer for public worship, but has been revised and re-worked to make it appropriate for use in churches, small groups, the family situation, or for personal quiet time devotions.

My church background was firmly in the camp of extemporary prayer. I started to write my prayers down due to nervousness and on the advice of my preaching mentor who insisted on careful preparation not only of the hymns, readings, and sermon, but also of the prayers. I have long since realised the value of having a resource to be used as a flexible launch pad for my own prayer life which I could use and adapt as I wished.

I hope that is how you will approach these simple aids to prayer. They have been deliberately written in an uncomplicated style and with language that seeks to illuminate the joy of prayer. I have also tried to ensure that they are written in the language we use in our daily conversations. The aim of this is designed to make them easier to 'pray' and not simply to 'read'.

David Clowes
Stockport, April 2020

TIME TO REFLECT ON THE SEASONS

IT'S WINTER

Lord, it's winter again and everywhere is cold and still.
When I look out of the window
I see the frost and the snow;
the grass and the trees sparkle like diamonds.
I can wear my warm coat, my gloves, and my hat
and feel quite snug,
though my face tingles and my breath looks like fog!
I put out breadcrumbs to make sure
the birds have been fed.
When I run and jump I can see
just where my feet have been.
Then it's time to go home, where a hot drink is waiting
and it's safe and warm.
It's good we have winter so everywhere can rest
and get ready for springtime.
Lord, you have shown us in Jesus
that your love is always warm

and wherever we go we can be sure you are there.
Amen.

SPRING IS HERE

Lord, winter has gone, and so has the snow;
each day is just a little warmer
and everywhere is brighter.
Lord, when I look at the trees and the hedgerows,
the gardens and the fields,
it makes me think that you have been busy making
them all fresh and clean.
Every year it's the same:
your world looks as if it has just been made!
Spring is here, the lambs
are jumping and dancing with joy,
and I feel I want to join in!
Lord, thank you for springtime—
it's like a picture that says,
'Like my world, you can begin again.'
Lord, I can't do that on my own
so I'm trusting you to help me—
just as you told me to. Amen.

SUMMERTIME

Will it always be like this?
Will I look back one day and remember
only long, hot summer days?

Lord, I want to say thank you
for all the lovely flowers.
They look so proud as they hold their heads high.
It is as if they are saying,
'Look at me, smell my perfume,
and enjoy my wonderful bright colours.'
Summer is the time to play outside with my friends,
to go to the seaside, and have lots of fun.
Summer is the time for laughter, for holidays,
and for enjoying just being alive in your world.
Thank you for summertime.
Help me to fill it with wonderful memories
that I can enjoy for the rest of my life. Amen.

IT'S AUTUMN AGAIN

Autumn is a unique time of year.
It's neither hurried and hot like summer should be,
nor is it like winter, with its chills and its cold.
It's certainly not spring,
for there's little new to be seen.
No, autumn is different—sort of stuck in between.
If the season were traffic lights,
then while winter means stop,
and spring and summer say go,
autumn is a kind of get-ready—either to stop or to go.
The harvest is gathered and all seems completed—
but there are the seeds of the new crop
that will be sown come next spring.

No, autumn is different, and some like it best.
There are leaves on the ground that rustle and snap
and when you walk through them
they get stuck in your shoes.
Autumn seems gentle, like nature thinking aloud;
as if, Lord, you are saying,
as you look back over the year,
'Well, that went well, just look what was achieved!'
So, Lord, thank you for autumn, its trees
and its bright-tinted leaves.
No artist could create that—
until you showed them how.
Thank you for time to reflect, and prepare. Amen.

TIME TO REFLECT ON OUR WALK WITH GOD

BUT MARY SAID YES

Lord, when you ask me to follow you
it would help if you told me where it might lead
and what it will cost me.
I would be ready to trust you
if I knew what you wanted.
If you made it a bit clearer, just what is involved,
then I might be more willing to go with you.

Lord, how can you expect anyone just to say yes;
to be ready to follow without really knowing
what it all means?
I know of the angel who came to Mary.
I have read of the amazing news he gave to her.
She must have been shocked
when he spoke of the baby

and probably felt like saying
it had nothing to do with her.
But Mary was different—she simply listened
and wondered what it all meant.
Then, when the angel had finished,
she simply said—yes.

Lord, Mary has taught me to trust you,
even when I don't understand,
and to walk along with you,
trusting that you know the way.
It is only when I accept your invitation,
and hold on to your hand,
that I can set out on the journey with you.

Lord, what matters is that *you* know
just where you are leading me and what it all means;
you know what it costs, and where it all ends.
So help me to trust you with the whole of my life
and give me the faith just to take the next step.
Amen.

THE RICH YOUNG MAN

What a choice he was given!
Follow Jesus and give everything away!
Am I really sure
what I would have done in his place?

His conversation with Jesus started out so well.
He wanted to know more about God
and how he could be sure that God was happy
with the way he lived.

He was such a serious young man.
At first he seemed to have more interest
in the things of heaven than the things of earth.

Somehow or other he appears
to have got the wrong end of the stick.
He seems to have got it into his head
that getting his life right with God
was something that depended on him
and what he could do himself;
he almost left God right out of the picture!

It was as though he thought that he could
work his own way to heaven
and eventually deserve his place there.
What he had yet to learn was
no one's place in heaven
can be won, earned, or deserved.
It can only be entered through the victory
Jesus has won by his death and resurrection.

The day had promised so much—
not a cloud in the sky.

The problems started
when Jesus told it to him straight.
He always seemed to know just who or what
people were putting first in their lives.

Lord, I praise you for Jesus' confrontation
with this young man
and the challenge this story has brought into my life.
I know that you will put your finger
on the things in my life
that are getting in the way of your being Lord,
if only I will let you.
Come, Lord Jesus, come. Amen.

CHRISTMAS—TOO MANY VOICES

Lord,
so many voices clamour for my attention
that I am confused
and sometimes I am not really sure
what Christmas means anymore.
I pray, help me this Christmas to listen to you.
Teach me again that through the Christ-child
you are telling me just how much I matter to you.
Show me that in Immanuel
you are promising to share all that life means to me.
Assure me that through the one who came
I can begin to know you as my Father.

Lord, I commit myself to be open to you
and ask that you will make a Christmas in my heart.
Through Jesus Christ,
who is the true Christmas. Amen.

WHY, LORD?

Lord, why is it that things happen the way they do?

When he picked up his brushes
to create a picture of what he saw all around him,
it was as if he was seeing the true colour
and shape of your world
for the very first time.

When she held her newborn son,
it was as if she was seeing life and its wonder
for the very first time.

When he sat with the dying
and shared something of the pain
and tears of the bereaved,
it was as if he was experiencing loss
for the very first time.

Lord, what does it mean when you tell us
that all things are made new in Christ?

The Lord says,
'My child, in my Son you can see my beauty,
experience my grief, and enter into the joy of life—
just as I planned it for you'. Amen.

TIME FOR CONFESSION

CHOOSING THE PATH

Forgive me, Father, for the times
when, like a lost sheep,
I have strayed from your path,
confident that I knew the way.
Pardon me that in my pride and wilfulness
I have wanted preferential treatment
at the expense of others.
When I try to get my own way
by harsh words, by anger, or by bullying,
teach me the meekness which patiently endures
and enable me to become one whose anger
is exercised on behalf of the oppressed.
When I am tempted to do nothing
in the face of clear human need,
because action will be costly or difficult,
set before me the example of Jesus.
I confess that I am tempted to leave your path

because I am afraid of the cost of the journey.
At these times, Lord, you gather me in,
you show me the way,
you equip me with the means to reach my goal,
and you invite my obedient response to your offer.
Give me the faith to make the journey
and, if the cross seems to lie ahead,
help me to see further than its apparent failure
to the victory that Christ won there
and to the eternal life that lies beyond. Amen.

SHUTTING OUT GOD

Father, I confess that I have listened for your voice
and have allowed the clamour of the world
and the busyness of my life
to drown your words of warning and challenge.
I confess that I have closed my eyes
to the signs of your presence
and your activity in the world.
I have closed my ears to your call
to share my plenty with the poor, the hungry,
and the starving.
I have made no time to be still
and know that you are God.
I have been too busy to read your Word and to pray.
I have been careless
when you called me to be careful.
I have been selfish

when you required me to give.
I have been hard-hearted
when you longed for me
to be gentle and understanding.
I have been resistant to change
when you wanted to make all things new.
I have neglected opportunities
to serve in your name,
to visit the sick, to give a cup of water in your name,
and to tell someone else of your love for us all.
Father, I am ashamed
and I know that I am not been living
as a true citizen of your kingdom.
Forgive my indifference, my selfishness,
and my disobedience.
Touch my heart, change my attitude,
and make my life new.
For Christ's sake. Amen.

OUT OF THE DARKNESS

Father, when I come to you
it is like walking out of darkness and into the light.
There are so many things,
so many experiences
that damage and spoil my life each day.
There are so many things that prevent me
from being the kind of person you meant me to be.
It would be so easy to come

simply to be held in your healing, re-creating love.
Father, by your Holy Spirit,
enable me to be made whole
by focusing on you
and allowing your praise to be at the centre
of all I say and do today.
In the name of Christ,
the one who makes all things new. Amen.

LORD, WE NEED YOUR LIGHT

Lord,
I confess
that I need your light
to heal my brokenness;
to restore my relationships;
to show me the way;
to cleanse and renew me;
to enable me to offer forgiveness to those
who have hurt me most;
and to receive the forgiveness
that you give to those who come
confessing their need of your light.

Lord,
I confess my need of your light,
trusting that you will light up my life
with your grace. Amen.

TIME TO REFLECT ON LIVING THE LIFE

LORD, I'M LEARNING TO LIVE ALONE

Lord,
I'm learning to live alone
after all those years
of balancing the demands
of work and home,
of family and friends.
The quiet space I once longed for
has become the barren desert of singleness
which breeds a sense of isolation.

Lord,
I still need to know
that I belong;
that I am valued;
that I have a part to play;

that I am still me;
that your presence fills my home
and your glory can flow
through every part of my life. Amen.

I WANT TO BE STILL

Lord, why won't they leave me alone?
I just want to be still,
to sit here quietly in your presence;
to enjoy a few brief moments
in your gentle, healing love.
But I live in a world addicted to making noise,
so my quiet space is under constant attack.
The telephone rings,
someone demands my attention;
the passing car pollutes my silence
with its unwanted, discordant sounds;
in every shop I am assaulted by unwanted music.

Lord, is that why you went away to the lonely places—
to find stillness in the presence of your Father?
Lord, teach me to find space
even in the hubbub and turmoil of my daily life;
to discover moments of tranquillity
in the most unlikely of places.
Help me to transform the frustration
of a traffic queue,
standing at the checkout,

and waiting for my turn in the doctor's surgery
into an oasis of stillness within,
as I allow Christ to be all things in all places to me.
Amen.

LOVING OUR NEIGHBOUR

Lord, I do not find it easy to like everyone,
let alone love them.
I do not love you with everything I have and am,
nor do I love my neighbour as myself.
I confess that I do not allow your love
to warm my heart towards others as you intended.
I do not offer your loving care as you had planned.
I confess that I am content to receive your love
but I am slow to share it.
Lord, forgive me my selfishness
and my self-centredness.
So transform my life by your love
that I may stand out as a living example
of your love and mercy.
Lord, convince me that
I am accepted, loved, and forgiven,
and by your Holy Spirit, send me out
to seek reconciliation with others
and to offer the love of Christ to all.
For his name's sake. Amen.

TIME FOR THANKFULNESS

THE LONG HOURS OF THE NIGHT

Lord,
thank you for being there
through the long hours of the night;
when things go well;
when the bottom drops out of my world;
when I choose to walk my own way;
and when I turn again and trust you
with the whole of my life. Amen.

LAUGHTER

Lord,
laughter is such a wonderful gift
and a very precious weapon
with which to face
the bumps and bangs of my daily life.

It is laughter that breaks the tension
and offers a way out of anger and frustration.
The ability to see the funny side
and the willingness to poke fun at myself
enriches the journey
and opens the way to hope and joy.

Lord,
I thank you for laughter
and the way it enables me
to see things from a different perspective.
I praise you for every good joke
that makes me laugh
and for every funny situation
that makes me smile.

Thank you for the laughter of children
that speaks of their innocence,
and their happy smiles
that fill me with hope and blessing.

I praise you for those
who help me to laugh and have fun
and I thank you for those
who have taught me to smile
even in the face of the storm.

Lord,
thank you for Jesus

and the laughter, peace, and joy
with which he is offering to fill my days.
I praise you that he is constantly
walking beside me
and that my laughter in him
will last from now
until I laugh with him
in the heaven of his love. Amen.

TIME TO REFLECT ON LEARNING NEW THINGS

A GLIMPSE OF GOD

I didn't know you were there, Lord.
It seemed from all that I had heard
that you were just a name;
a heavenly being; a prop for the weak;
a figment of the human imagination.
When I said my prayers
I never really expected you to answer;
how could you, if you were not really there?

But now—now it's all different.
Just the other day it was as if
I had actually caught a glimpse of you!
And now the God I didn't know I meet everywhere.
I see you in the sunrise and in the sunset.
I meet you in the kindness of friends

and in the compassion of strangers.
I recognise your face in the nameless multitude
who rush to respond to the latest appeal
for the hungry and starving.

I hear your voice when I read your Word
and find you near when I turn to prayer.
When I am alone and have lost my way,
I rediscover your presence, even in the darkness.
When the bottom drops out of my world
and all that mattered
seems to slip through my fingers,
your peace and your joy hold me in your grace.
When I have more questions than I have answers
and my heart and my mind are in turmoil,
I catch a glimpse of you in the face of Jesus,
who comes and promises to hold my hand,
now and for all eternity.

For now, I must be satisfied with a glimpse of you—
one day, by grace, I shall see you face to face. Amen.

TEACH ME, LORD

Lord, in a world of rushing feet, teach me to be still.
When I am surrounded by greed
and materialistic excess,
teach me to be content.
In the midst of those with angry

or demanding voices,
teach me to be gentle and wise.
When those around me have eyes and ears
for their own desires,
teach me to remember the needs of others.
In the crush of self-centredness and self-sufficiency,
teach me to stand aside and trust in you.
When those with whom I share each day
at work or in the world
see no further than what can be seen
or touched or understood,
teach me to focus on you
and to walk in faith—always. Amen.

LACK OF EXPECTATION

Father, you have promised me so much,
and yet I expect so little to happen.
You have promised to be with me always,
but I enter each day and each situation
in fear and trepidation.
You have promised to hold me
and heal my brokenness,
but I find it hard to put my whole trust in you.
You have promised
that I shall be with you in heaven,
but I continue to live as if death is the end.
You have promised to use me to lead other people
to a knowledge of your love in Christ,

but my witness is feeble and my example
deprives my neighbour of hope and of heaven.
Father, our Father, cleanse my heart and mind.
Renew my faith and my hold on you.
May your Spirit transform me into
a vibrant channel of your grace. Amen.

THE IMAGES WE DESIRE

Lord, you told me to have no graven images,
but I have surrounded myself with pictures
of those who are famous as the gods of success.
I fix my eyes on the symbols
of wealth and material possessions—
they are my images of worthwhile achievement.
I breathe in the atmosphere
of indulgence and indifference
as if these were the mark of goals worth pursuing.
I seek to follow in the steps of those
I consider my role models
and listen attentively to those
I have long sought to emulate.
Lord, too often these are the gods that I worship
and, although I am quick to deny it,
I still allow them the place in my devotion
that was always meant to be yours.

Lord, you are the King of creation
and sovereign over all things—

there is nothing and no one your equal.
Lord, you are the King of creation
and sovereign over all things—
you are the one before whom nothing existed.
Lord, you are the King of creation
and sovereign over all things—
and when time is no more you are still God. Amen.

DENIAL OF LOVE

Lord, I have known your presence,
but my life and my words and my deeds
deny that I have ever met you.
I have experienced your love,
but I have not allowed it to flow through me
to my neighbour.
I have witnessed your life-changing grace
in my own life,
but through my excuses and my timidity
I prevent others receiving it too.
I have fed on the love of Christ
and been filled with the power of his Spirit,
but I still fail to demonstrate your love for others,
and my worship and service are a poor offering
to make to such a wonderful God.
Forgive me, Lord, and transform my life.
Forgive me my denial of your love
and call me again to your service. Amen.

WE ARE DEAF

Lord, you speak, but I am deaf.
You call, but I do not want to listen.
You challenge me, but I close my ears.
You hold out your hand to guide and to lift me,
but I turn away from you.
You reach out to give me your comfort,
but I am too self-confident to receive it.
You join me on my journey,
but I do not recognise you.
You try to change the direction of my life,
but I think that I know best.
You warm my cold heart,
you inspire my faith,
and you forgive me again and again,
and I am amazed.
Lord, open my heart to your grace
and renew my hope and my faith
in Christ our Lord. Amen.

WHY PETER? (WHY ME?)

Lord, there are many things in this world
that I don't understand.
There are many things
that are beyond my comprehension.
There are many things
about which I wish I knew more.

My head is full of questions
for which I have no answers;
things that puzzle me as I search for a solution.

Lord, I would love to know: why Peter?
What was it about him
that was so special, so different?
What was it about Peter
that made you reject the others
and choose him to be your disciple?
What did you see in him
that marked him out from the crowd?
Lord, I would love to know: why Peter?

Lord, I would love to know: why Peter?
Why was he the one who first voiced
the word of faith and named you his Lord?
What was it that he saw in you
that touched and transformed
this uneducated, illiterate, working-class fisherman?
How was he changed into the spokesperson
for all your disciples—then and now
and for all time to come?
Why Peter, Lord?
Why was he the one on whom
you committed yourself
to build the new people of God?
It wasn't as if his faith was so very deep

or that he really understood who you were
or what it all meant.
So why Peter, Lord?

Why Peter, Lord—why did he get it all wrong?
How did he manage to miss
the signs of Judas planning his betrayal
and how did he fail to protect his Lord?
How could he not understand
why you were washing his feet?
How could he fall asleep in the garden
at the moment you had asked him to pray?
Why Peter, Lord?
How could he deny all knowledge of you—
he who had confessed you as Lord?
I know he wept over his failure,
all done in the face of a hostile crowd.
But why Peter, Lord?

Why Peter, Lord?
Why was he the one to run to the tomb
and discover that you had been raised
and the victory over death had been won?
Though if the truth be known,
he didn't understand a great deal
of all that it really meant.
Why was it Peter who found the grave empty
and that there was no body there?
How was it that it was Peter

who was faced with your threefold challenge
to care for your lambs and your sheep?
And why was it possible for this man,
who was known to have feet made of clay,
to declare on the day of Pentecost
the truth that Jesus is Lord?
Why, I ask—why Peter, Lord?

What I really mean, and what I really want to ask,
is not why Peter, but why me, Lord?
Why did you choose me and use me and fill me?
Why did you call me and shape me and send me?
Why did you love me and restore me?
Why did you offer yourself as my Saviour and Lord?

For Peter and for me, the answer is grace.
Your undeserved love has made me your own
and, by your Spirit, Peter and I have received
all the power we needed
to declare to all who will hear
that Jesus is Lord, to the glory of God the Father.
Amen.

LORD, TOUCH EVEN ME

Lord,
touch my mind, that my thoughts
may be worthy of you;
touch my mouth, that I may speak of your love;

touch my hands, that I may serve in your name;
touch my heart, that I may love the unlovely;
touch my feet, that I may always follow Christ;
touch my promises, that I may be faithful to you;
touch my hopes,
that they might be filled with your grace;
touch my fears, that I might be strengthened anew;
touch my plans,
that they might be focused on your glory;
touch my love,
that it might be a true reflection of your compassion;
touch my giving,
that it might find its source in Christ's sacrifice;
touch my life, that all I say or do may bring you joy.
Amen.

THE LORD SAID

Lord,
you said, 'Come' and I walked away.
You said, 'Follow' and I chose my way.
You said, 'Trust' and I turned my back on you.
You said, 'Hope' and I was full of despair.
You said, 'I am here' and I didn't want to know.
You said, 'I love you' and you showed me
your hands and your side
and I didn't know what to say.
You reached out to hold me,

to draw me into your love
and, at last, I was able to say, 'Thank you.'
You said, 'You are forgiven and you are accepted'
and I wept with joy.
You said, 'I am the Lord'
and I knelt before you,
lost in wonder, love, and praise. Amen.

IT'S NOT TOO LATE

Father,
I looked in my heart
and I was ashamed of the thoughts
that I found there.
I listened to my voice
and I was embarrassed by the things I was saying.
I was aware of the people I have hurt
and I felt guilty to have damaged my neighbour.
I stood feeling uncomfortable in your holy presence,
reluctant to acknowledge where I had gone wrong.

Then you reached out in love
and you showed me the cross.
You dealt with the pages of my days
that had been marked by deliberate mistakes
and you opened a new page and promised me hope.
You held me so close in your word of love
and offered me peace as I responded in joy.

Once more you came near to me
and in a whisper of grace
you offered me hope when you declared:
it's not too late to begin again! Amen.

IT IS NOT MINE

Lord,
it is not mine to abuse,
but in my greed
that is what I am doing.

It is not mine to consume,
but I am stealing
the future hope of generations.

It is not mine to act recklessly,
but I am closing my ears
to the warnings of truth.

It is not mine to deny
all creatures, great and small,
the future you intended.

It is not mine to act
as if I am the lord of the earth
rather than a servant of the King.

Lord,
I kneel before you
and in repentance confess
that, 'The earth is the Lord's
and everything in it'. Amen.

I STAND AMAZED!

Lord,
I stood and I was enthralled
by the power of the waterfall;
I was entranced
by the beauty of the ever-changing sunset;
I was held spellbound
as the songs of the birds filled the air;
I was utterly overwhelmed
by the sublime majesty of the blue whale;
I experienced a tremendous feeling of joy
at the gentle beauty of the wildflower meadow;
I had no words to express the wonder
as the mother held a newborn baby.

I thought I had seen
all that your creation could offer
until I saw the 'earth-rise' picture of our blue planet.
It was then that I was moved with that vision
of our fragile world
to truly declare, 'The earth is the Lord's'.
All praise to the sovereign over all things. Amen.

A WORLD TRANSFORMED?

A world transformed, Lord?
But there is nothing wrong with your world—
you said it was very good!

We are surrounded
by the colours, designs, and sounds
that make this blue planet
such a perfect home for us all.

Lord, it isn't the world,
it is me that needs to be transformed.
It was only when your grace
removed the cataracts of self-interest from my eyes
and your love touched
the hardness of self-centredness in my heart
that I really understood the damage that
my words, my deeds, and my lifestyle
are doing to your world.

So, Lord, come each day
and transform my whole being
that you may transform your world—
even through me. Amen.

THE WORDS I USE

Father, I am full of words—
but they are often words of anger, bitterness,

and jealousy.
I use my words
to hurt others,
to spoil relationships,
and to build barriers between us.
I use words to make myself sound compassionate,
but my thoughts are selfish
and my intentions self-centred.
I use words to criticise others,
to belittle, and to gossip,
hurting you and my neighbour.
I have no right to ask for forgiveness
and there is no earthly reason
why you should cleanse and renew me.
I simply have faith that in Christ you will.
Father, speak the word of hope, mercy, cleansing,
and renewal,
and give me the power and commission
to offer them to others.
In the name of Christ, whose name is love. Amen.

TIME TO REFLECT ON GOD

YOU ARE ALL (PSALM 16:5 GNB)

Lord,
I am on my knees—
battered by the insinuations
and the falsehoods all around us;
the messages that are planted in my mind
and the whispered half-truths
that rob me of my peace and contentment.

Every day and every hour,
every minute and every second,
from anywhere and everywhere,
our consumer-driven society
undermines my confidence
in who and what I am.
It mocks my expectations
of hope, joy, peace, and wholeness.
It is assumed that I should fill my days

with the material symbols
our society equates with success.

But, Lord, I have an emptiness within
that not all the world's most sublime riches
or mountain of possessions can ever satisfy.

Then in the depths of my longings
and in the centre of my frustration
your servant speaks the word of hope
and the message that has the power to challenge
all my false assumptions.

The psalmist reminds me that
you, Lord, are all I need
and ultimately you are all I have,
and all that offers life now
and for ever. Amen.

LORD, YOU GAVE ME TODAY

Lord, you gave me today. I am glad to receive it.
You gave it to me as a free gift
and not as a reward for how I made use of yesterday.

Lord, you gave me today.
It came from your hand,
fresh and new, clean and unspoilt.
Lord, you gave me today.

It was just the right shape and size
for all you planned for me to do in and with it.

Lord, you gave me today.
Twenty-four hours to fill
with love, joy, peace, hope, and service.
Lord, you gave me today, only today.
But I forgot and filled it with so many things
that there was no time or space for you.

Lord, you gave me today.
But too often it is spoilt with thoughts
and memories of yesterday.
Sometimes my mind is filled
with the anger, the bitterness, the weakness,
the broken promises, and the mistakes
of the day you gave me that will never return.

Lord, you gave me today.
But I can't rest; peace is a long-forgotten dream
and I am afraid about the tomorrow
you have yet to grant me.
Tomorrow may never be mine,
but I still worry about what it will bring
and how well I will cope.

Lord, you gave me today.
Help me to receive it as the gracious gift that it is.
Lord, you gave me today.

Forgive my misuse of yesterday
and, by your Holy Spirit,
enable me to live your precious gift of today
to the full and for you and your glory.

Lord, you gave me today. I give it back to you now.
It is all I have to give,
and it is my sacrifice of praise and thanksgiving.
Amen.

OPEN MY EYES

Lord,
open my eyes to see your world;
open my ears to hear the cry of the poor;
open my mind to learn more of your love;
open my mouth to speak of your grace;
open my thoughts to make more room for you;
open my will to obey you in all things;
open my heart to invite you to come in. Amen.

YOU GAVE ME LIFE

Lord,
you gave me life—
help me to live it for you;
you gave me hope—
help me to share it with my neighbour;
you gave me joy—

help me to enrich the lives of others;
you gave me your love—
help me to give your love away
to everyone I meet today. Amen.

MY HIGHEST THOUGHT

Lord,
you are my highest thought
and you meet my deepest need.
You challenge me to walk in your narrow way
and open my mind to grasp something
of the width of your grace.
You remind me each day how short my life really is
and you offer me your peace and love,
whose length reaches to the end of eternity.
For the height, depth, and length of your love,
I kneel to give you thanks
and I rise to offer you my praise.
In the name of Jesus,
whose arms, stretched wide on the cross,
proved the width of your love. Amen.

I LIE AWAKE

Lord,
I lie awake
and I think of all I have done
with my life today.

I remember the things
I have left undone;
the people I have let down;
the times I have failed, Lord.
I have come to you now
because I know that you
are simply longing to forgive me.
Help me to begin again. Amen.

LORD, I THINK

Lord,
I think of the things I've planned
and the dreams I've had.
I remember
the people I have known—
those who have cared,
the ones who have loved.
Some memories still hurt.
Lord, grant me your healing grace
and refresh my life with your love. Amen.

THE JOURNEYS

Lord, I think of the journeys I have made
and the places I have visited.
I return in my mind to the times of joy
that have enriched my days
and those experiences of God's presence

that have meant so much.
Give me the assurance that you will go on sharing
every journey I make today
and my journey home to you. Amen.

MEMORIES

Lord, I think of those memories
that are precious,
and those whose love
is still filling my life.
I remember the times
I have spent with those
who matter most to me.
For the gift of memory
and the assurance
that I am always in your care,
I give you heartfelt thanks and praise. Amen.

THE END OF THE YEAR

Lord, I think of the year that is past—
the things you have done,
and the things I have failed to do.

Lord, I think of the year that is past—
the things that have been important to me
and for which I want to give thanks and praise.

Lord, I think of the year that is past—
the things I want to leave behind,
the things that have hurt me too deeply for words.

Lord, I think of the year that is past—
those moments when I knew you were with me
giving me courage, peace,
and a love whose depth cannot be measured.

Lord, I think of the year that is past—
the uncertainty of what it holds
and what it will mean for me and my life.

Lord, I think of the year that is past—
the hopes I have and the good things I am longing
for you to do in my life.

Lord, I think of the year that is past—
the opportunities for witness and service
and the promise of the Holy Spirit to equip me
for giving, caring, and loving.

Lord, I think of the year that is past—
this is the moment for me to thank you for it
and to place it firmly in the hands of the one who is
almighty. Amen.

LORD, HELP ME TO BE

Lord,
help me to be your voice to those seeking answers;
help me to be your comfort to those who are alone;
help me to be your eyes
to see those who have been forgotten;
help me to be your feet
to those who are longing to be visited;
help me to be your hands
to those who simply want to be hugged;
help me to be your ears
to those who need to know they have been heard;
help me to be your compassion
to those who feel empty and worthless;
help me to be your song
to those who are seeking hope;
help me to be your laughter
to those who need to learn to smile again;
help me to be your presence
to those to whom you are sending me.
Lord, come live in me and help me
to be the me you always meant me to be,
that I may be as Jesus to everyone I meet. Amen.

ABOUT THE AUTHOR

David Clowes, born in Ellesmere Port, left school at fifteen following a secondary modern education. In 1965 he committed his life to Christ at Heaton Mersey Methodist and in 1967 he received God's call into the Methodist ministry. He trained at Hartley Victoria College and gained a degree in theology at Manchester University.

David served in a number of churches in the northwest of England before retiring in 2010 after thirty-five years in active ministry. His first book, *500 Prayers for All Occasions*, began as a spiritual exercise during a sabbatical. This was followed by *500 More Prayers for All Occasions*. His third book of prayers, *500 Prayers for the Christian Year*, is based on scriptures from the Revised Common Lectionary.

David is married to Angela, and they have two married sons, a foster son, and four grandchildren.